Thomas Paine

A Letter to the Earl of Shelburne, now Marquis of Lansdowne, on His Speech

July 10, 1782

Thomas Paine

A Letter to the Earl of Shelburne, now Marquis of Lansdowne, on His Speech
July 10, 1782

ISBN/EAN: 9783744691727

Printed in Europe, USA, Canada, Australia, Japan

Cover: Foto ©ninafisch / pixelio.de

More available books at **www.hansebooks.com**

A
LETTER

TO THE

EARL OF SHELBURNE,

NOW

MARQUIS OF LANSDOWNE.

A

LETTER

TO THE

EARL OF SHELBURNE,

NOW

MARQUIS of LANSDOWNE,

ON HIS

S. P. E. E. C. H,

JULY 10, 1782,

RESPECTING THE ACKNOWLEDGEMENT OF

AMERICAN INDEPENDENCE.

———————

By THOMAS PAINE,

Secretary for Foreign Affairs to Congrefs in the American
War, and Author of COMMON SENSE, a LETTER to
the ABBE RAYNAL, RIGHTS of MAN, &c.

═══════════════

D U B L I N:

PRINTED FOR G. BURNET, P. BYRNE, P. WOGAN, W.
SLEATER, A. GRUEBER, J. MOORE, J. JONES, G.
DRAPER, W. JONES, R. WHITE, R. M'ALLISTER,
J. RICE AND M. O'LEARY.

M.DCC.XCI.

‘A

L E T T E R, &c.

My Lord,

A SPEECH which has been printed in several of the Britiſh and New-York Newſpapers, as coming from your Lordſhip, in anſwer to one from the Duke of Richmond of the 10th of July laſt, contains expreſſions and opinions ſo new and ſingular, and ſo enveloped in myſterious reaſoning, that I addreſs this publication to you, for the purpoſe of giving them a free and candid examination. The ſpeech I allude to is in theſe words:

" His Lordſhip ſaid, it had been men-
" tioned in another place, that he had been
" guilty of inconſiſtence. To clear himſelf
" of this, he aſſerted that he ſtill held the
" ſame principles in reſpect to American
" Independence which he at firſt imbibed.
" He had been, and yet was of opinion,
" whenever the Parliament of Great Britain
" acknowledges that point, the ſun of Eng-
" land's glory is ſet for ever. Such were
" the ſentiments he poſſeſſed on a former
" day, and ſuch the ſentiments he conti-
" nued to hold at this hour. It was the
" opinion of Lord Chatham, as well as many
" able ſtateſmen. Other noble Lords, how-
" ever, think differently; and as the majority
" of the Cabinet ſupport them, he acquieſced
" in the meaſure, diſſenting from the idea;
" and the point is ſettled for bringing the mat-
" ter into the full diſcuſſion of Parliament,
" where it will be candidly, fairly, and im-
partially

" partially debated. The Independence of
" America would end in the ruin of Eng-
" land ; and that a peace patched up with
" France would give that proud enemy the
" means of yet trampling on this country.
" The fun of England's glory he wifhed not
" to fee fet for ever; he looked for a fpark
" at leaft to be left, which might in time light
" us up to a new day. But if Independence
" was to be granted, if Parliament deemed
" that meafure prudent, he forefaw in his
" own mind that England was undone. He
" wifhed to God that he had been deputed
" to Congrefs, that he might plead the caufe
" of that country as well as of this, and that
" he might exercife whatever powers he
" poffeffed as an orator, to fave both from
" ruin, in a conviction to Congrefs, that, if
" their Independence was figned, their liber-
" ties were gone for ever.

" PEACE,

"PEACE, his Lordſhip added, was a de-
" firable object, but it muſt be an honour-
" able peace, and not an humiliating one,
" dictated by France, or infiſted on by Ame-
" rica. It was very true, this kingdom was
" not in a flouriſhing ſtate, it was impo-
" veriſhed by war. But if we were not
" rich, it was evident that France was poor.
" If we were ſtraitened in our finances,
" the enemy were exhauſted in their re-
" fources. This was a great empire; it
' abounded with brave men, who were able
" and willing to fight in a common cauſe;
" the language of humiliation ſhould not,
" therefore, be the language of Great Britain.
" His Lordſhip ſaid, that he was not aſha-
" med nor afraid of thoſe expreſſions going
" to America. There were numbers, great
" numbers there, who were of the ſame way
" of thinking, in reſpect to that country
                                        " being

" being dependent on this, and who, with
" his Lordſhip, perceived ruin and inde-
" pendence linked together."

Thus far the ſpeech; on which I remark,
—That his Lordſhip is a total ſtranger to
the mind and ſentiments of America; that
he has wrapped himſelf up in fond deluſion,
that ſomething leſs than Independence may,
under his Adminiſtration, be accepted; and
he wiſhes himſelf ſent to Congreſs, to prove
the moſt extraordinary of all doctrines, which
is, that INDEPENDENCE, the ſublimeſt of all
human conditions, is loſs of liberty.

In anſwer to which we may ſay, that in
order to know what the contrary word DE-
PENDENCE means, we have only to look back
to thoſe years of ſevere humiliation, when
the mildeſt of all petitions could obtain no

B   other

other notice than the haughtieft of all infults; and when the bafe terms of unconditional fubmiffion were demanded, or un-
diftinguifhable deftruction threatened. It is
nothing to us that the Miniftry have been
changed, for they may be changed again.
The guilt of Government is the crime of a
whole country; and the nation that can,
though but for a moment, think and act as
England has done, can never afterwards be
believed or trufted. There are cafes in
which it is as impoffible to reftore character
to life, as it is to recover the dead. It is a
phœnix that can expire but once, and from
whofe afhes there is no refurrection. Some
offences are of fuch a flight compofition,
that they reach no farther than the temper,
and are created or cured by a thought. But
the fin of England has ftruck the heart of
America,

America, and nature has not left it in our power to fay we can forgive.

You R Lordſhip wiſhes for an opportunity to plead before Congreſs *the cauſe of England and America, and to ſave, as you ſay, both from ruin.*

THAT the country, which, for more than ſeven years, has fought our deſtruction, ſhould now cringe to ſolicit our protection, is adding the wretchedneſs of diſgrace to the miſery of diſappointment; and if England has the leaſt ſpark of ſuppoſed honour left, that ſpark muſt be darkened by aſking, and extinguiſhed by receiving, the ſmalleſt favour from America: for the criminal who owes his life to the grace and mercy of the injured, is more executed by living than he who dies.

B 2   BUT

BUT a thoufand pleadings, even from your Lordfhip, can have no effect Honour, intereft, and every fenfation of the heart, would plead againft you. We are a people who think not as you think, and what is equally true, you cannot feel as we feel. The fituations of the two countries are exceedingly different. We have been the feat of war: you have feen nothing of it. The moft wanton deftruction has been committed in our fight; the moft infolent barbarity has been acted on our feelings. We can look round and fee the remains of burnt and deftroyed houfes, once the fair fruit of hard induftry, and now the ftriking monuments of Britifh brutality. We walk over the dead whom we loved, in every part of America, and remember by whom they fell. There is fcarcely a village but brings to life fome melancholy thought, and reminds us of what

we

we have fuffered, and of thofe we have loft by the inhumanity of Britain. A thoufand images arife to us, which, from fituation, you cannot fee, and are accompanied by as many ideas which you cannot know; and therefore your fuppofed fyftem of reafoning would apply to nothing, and all your expec-tations die of themfelves.

THE queftion, whether England fhall ac-cede to the Independence of America, and which your Lordfhip fays is to undergo a parliamentary difcuffion, is fo very fimple, and compofed of fo few cafes, that it fcarcely needs a debate.

IT is the only way out of an expenfive and ruinous war, which has now no objeɊ, and without which acknowledgement there can be no peace.

BUT

But your Lordſhip ſays, " *The ſun of Great Britain will ſet whenever ſhe acknowledges the Independence of America.*" Whereas the metaphor would have been ſtrictly juſt, to have left the ſun wholly out of the figure, and have aſcribed her not acknowledging it to the influence of the moon.

But the expreſſion, if true, is the greateſt confeſſion of diſgrace that could be made, and furniſhes America with the higheſt notions of ſovereign independent importance. Mr. Wedderburne, about the year 1776, made uſe of an idea of much the ſame kind, —" *Relinquiſh America!*" ſays he—*What is* " *it but to deſire a giant to ſhrink ſpontaneouſly* " *into a dwarf.*"

Alas! are thoſe people who call themſelves Engliſhmen, of ſo little internal conſequence,

quence, that when America is gone, or shuts her eyes upon them, their sun is set, they can shine no more, but grope about in obscurity, and contract into insignificant animals? Was America, then, the giant of the empire, and England only her dwarf in waiting? Is the case so strangely altered, that those who once thought we could not live without them, now declare they cannot exist without us? Will they tell to the world, and that from their first Minister of State, that America is their all in all; that it is by her importance only they can live, and breathe. and have a being? Will they, who threatened to bring us to their feet, now cast themselves at ours, and own that without us they are not a nation? Are they become so unqualified to debate on Independence, that they have lost all idea of it in themselves, and are calling to the rocks and mountains of America

to

to cover their infignificance? Or, if America is loft, is it manly to fob over it like a child for its rattle, and invite the laughter of the world by declarations of difgrace? Surely, the more confiftent conduct would be, to bear it without complaint; and to fhew that England, without America, can preferve her independence, and a fuitable rank with other European Powers. You were not contented while you had her, and to weep for her now is childifh.

But Lord Shelburne thinks that fomething may yet be done. What that fomething is, or how it is to be accomplifhed, is a matter in obfcurity. By arms there is no hope. The experience of nearly eight years, with the expence of an hundred million pounds fterling, and the lofs of two armies, muft pofitively decide that point. Befides,

the

the Britifh have loft their interest in America
with the difaffected. , Every part of it has
been tried. There is no new fcene left for
delufion : and the thoufands who have been
ruined by adhering to them, and have now
to quit the fettlements they had acquired,
and be conveyed like tranfports to cultivate
the deferts of Auguftine and Nova Scotia;
has put an end to all farther expectations of
aid.

If you caft your eyes on the people of
England, what have they to confole themfelves with for the millions expended ? or,
what encouragement is there left to continue
throwing good money after bad ? America
can carry on the war for ten years longer,
and all the charges of government included,
for lefs than you can defray the charges of
war and government for one year. And I,

who

who know both countries, know well, that the people of America can afford to pay their share of the expence much better than the people of England can. Besides, it is their own estates and property, their own rights, liberties and government, they are defending; and were they not to do it, they would deserve to lose all, and none would pity them. The fault would be their own, and their punishment just.

THE British army in America care not how long the war lasts. They enjoy an easy and indolent life. They fatten on the folly of one country and the spoils of another; and, between their plunder and their pay, may go home rich. But the case is very different with the labouring farmer, the working tradesman, and the necessitous poor in England, the sweat of whose brow goes

day

day after day to feed, in prodigality and floth, the army that is robbing both them and us. Removed from the eye of the country that fupports them, and diftant from the govern‑ ment that employs them, they cut and carve for themfelves, and there is none to call them to account.

But England will be ruined, fays Lord Shelburne, if America is independent.

Then, I fay, is England already ruined, for America is already independent: and if Lord Shelburne will not allow this, he im‑ mediately denies the fact which he infers. Befides, to make England the mere creature of America, is paying too great a compliment to us, and too little to himfelf.

C 2   But

BUT the declaration is a rhapfody of in-
confiftence. For to fay, as Lord Shelburne
has numberlefs times faid, that the war
againft America is ruinous, and yet to continue the profecution of that ruinous war for
the purpofe of avoiding ruin, is a language
which cannot be underftood. Neither is it
poffible to fee how the Independence of
America is to accomplifh the ruin of England after the war is over, and yet not effect
it before. America cannot be more independent of her, nor a greater enemy to her,
hereafter than fhe is now; nor England de-
rive lefs advantages from her than at prefent:
why then is ruin to follow in the beft ftate
of the cafe, and not in the worft! And if not
in the worft, why is it to follow at all?

THAT a nation is to be ruined by peace
and commerce, and fourteen or fifteen millions

lions a-year lefs expences than before, is a new doctrine in politics. We have heard much clamour of national favings and œconomy; but furely the true œconomy would be, to fave the whole charge of a filly, foolifh, and headftrong war; becaufe, compared with this, all other retrenchments are bawbles and trifles.

But is it poffible that Lord Shelburne can be ferious in fuppofing the leaft advantage can be obtained by arms, or that any advantage can be equal to the expence, or the danger of attempting it? Will not the capture of one army after another fatisfy him, but all muft become prifoners? Muft England ever be the fport of hope and the dupe of delufion? Sometimes our currency was to fail; another time our army was to difband: then whole provinces were to revolt. Such a General

said

said this and that; another wrote so and so. Lord Chatham was of this opinion; and Lord Somebody else of another. To-day 20,000 Ruffians and 20 Ruffian ships of the line were to come; to-morrow the Emprefs was abused without mercy or decency.— Then the Emperor of Germany was to be bribed with a million of money, and the King of Pruffia was to do wonderful things. At one time it was, Lo here! and then it was, Lo there! Sometimes this Power, and fometimes that Power, was to engage in the war, juft as if the whole world was as mad and foolifh as Britain. And thus, from year to year, has every ftraw been catched at, and every Will-with-a-Wifp led them a new dance.

THIS year a ftill newer folly is to take place. Lord Shelburne wifhes to be fent

to

to Congrefs, and he thinks that fomething may be done.

ARE not the repeated declarations of Congrefs, and which all America fupports, that they will not even hear any propofals whatever, until the unconditional and unequivocal Independence of America is recognifed; are not, I fay, thefe declarations anfwer enough?

BUT for England to receive any thing from America now, after fo many infults, injuries, and outrages, acted towards us, would fhew fuch a fpirit of meannefs in her, that we could not but defpife her for accepting it. And fo far from Lord Shelburne coming here to folicit it, it would be the greateft difgrace we could do them to offer it. England would appear a wretch indeed,

at

at this time of day, to aſk or owe any thing
to the bounty of America. Has not the
name of Engliſhman blots enough upon it,
without inventing more? Even Lucifer would
ſcorn to reign in Heaven by permiſſion, and
yet an Engliſhman can creep for only an
entrance into America. Or has a land of
Liberty ſo many charms, that to be a door-
keeper in it is better than to be an Engliſh
Miniſter of State?

But what can this expected ſomething
be? or, if obtained, what can it amount to,
but new diſgraces, contentions, and quar-
rels? The people of America have for years
accuſtomed themſelves to think and ſpeak
ſo freely and contemptuouſly of Engliſh
authority, and the inveteracy is ſo deeply
rooted, that a perſon inveſted with any authority from that country, and attempting

to

to exercife it here, would have the life of a toad under a harrow, They would look on him as an interloper, to whom their compaffion permitted a refidence. He would be no more than the Mungo of the farce; and if he difliked that, he muft fet off. It would be a ftation of degradation, debafed by our pity, and defpifed by our pride, and would place England in a more contemptible fituation than any fhe has yet fuffered by the war. We have too high an opinion of ourfelves, ever to think of yielding again the leaft obedience to outlandifh authority, and for a thoufand reafons, England would be the laft country in the world to yield it to. She has been treacherous, and we know it. Her character is gone, and we have feen the funeral.

D

SURELY

"Surely she loves to fish in troubled waters, and drink the cup of contention, or she would not now think of mingling her affairs with those of America: It would be like a foolish dotard taking to his arms the bride that despises him, or who has placed on his head the ensigns of her disgust. It is kissing the hand that boxes his ears, and proposing to renew the exchange. The thought is as servile as the war was wicked, and shews the last scene of the drama as inconsistent as the first."

As America is gone, the only act of manhood is to *let her go.* Your Lordship had no hand in the separation, and you will gain no honour by temporising politics. Besides, there is something so exceedingly whimsical, unsteady, and even insincere in the prefent conduct of England, that fhe exhibits herfelf in the moft difhonourable colours.

On the fecond of Auguft laft General Carleton and Admiral Digby wrote to General Wafhington in thefe words :

" THE refolution of the Houfe of Com-
" mons of the 27th of February laft have
" been placed in your Excellency's hands,
" and intimations given at the fame time,
" that farther pacific meafures were likely
" to follow. Since which, until the prefent
" time, we have had no direct communica-
" tions from England; but a mail is now
" arrived, which brings us very important
" information. We are acquainted, Sir,
" *by authority*, that negotiations for a gene-
" ral peace have already commenced at

D 2   " Paris,

" Paris, and that Mr. Grenville is invested
" with full powers to treat with all the
" parties at war, and is now at Paris in the
" execution of his commiſſion.   And we are
" farther, Sir, made acquainted, "*that his*
" *Majeſty, in order to remove any obſtacles to*
" *that peace which he ſo ardently wiſhes to*
" *reſtore, has commanded his Miniſters to direct*
" *Mr. Grenville, that the Independence of the*
" *Thirteen United provinces, ſhould be propoſed*
" *by him in the firſt inſtance, inſtead of making*
" *it a condition of a general treaty.*"

Now, taking your preſent meaſures into
view, and comparing them with the declaration in this Letter, pray, what is the word
of your King, or his Miniſters, or the Parliament, good for?   Muſt we not look upon
you as a confederated body of faithleſs, treacherous men, whoſe aſſurances are fraud,
                                             and

and their language deceit? What opinion
can we poffibly form of you, but that you
are a loft, abandoned, profligate nation, who
fport even with your own character, and are
to be held by nothing but the bayonet or the
halter?

To fay, after this, *that the fun of Great
Britain will be fet whenever fhe acknowledges
the Independence of America*, when the not
doing it is the unqualified lie of Government, can be no other than the language of
ridicule, the jargon of inconfiftency. There
were thoufands in America who predicted
the delufion, and looked upon it as a trick
of treachery, to take us from our guard, and
draw off our attention from the only fyftem
of finance, by which we can be called, or
deferve to be called, a fovereign, independent people. The fraud, on your part,
might

might be worth attempting, but the sacrifice
to obtain it is too high.

THERE were others who credited the af-
furance, becaufe they thought it impoffible
that men who had their characters to efta-
blifh, would begin it with a lie. The profecution of the war by the former Miniftry
was favage and horrid, fince, which it has
been mean, trickifh, and delufive. The one
went greedily into the paffion of revenge,
the other into the fubtleties of low contri-
vance; till, between the crimes of both,
there is fcarcely left a man in America, be
he Whig or Tory, who does not defpife or
deteft the conduct of Britain.

THE management of Lord Shelburne,
whatever may be his views, is a caution to
us, and muft be to the world, never to regard
British

British affurances. A perfidy fo notorious cannot be hid. It ftands even in the public papers of New York, with the names of Carleton and Digby affixed to it. It is a proclamation that the King of England is not to be believed: that the fpirit of lying is the governing principle of the Miniftry. It is holding up the character of the Houfe of Commons to public infamy, and warning all men not to credit them. Such is the confequence which Lord Shelburne's management has brought upon his country.

AFTER the authorifed declarations contained in Carleton and Digby's letter, you ought, from every motive of honour, policy, and prudence, to have fulfillled them, whatever might have been the event. It was the leaft atonement you could poffibly make to America, and the greateft kindnefs you could

do

do to yourſelves; for you will ſave millions
by a general peace, and you will loſe as many
by continuing the war.

COMMON SENSE.

Philadelphia,
October 29, 1782.

P. S. The manuſcript copy of this letter
is ſent your Lordſhip, by the way of our
Head Quarters, to New York, incloſing a
late pamphlet of mine, addreſſed to the Abbe
Reynal, which will ſerve to give your Lordſhip ſome idea of the principles and ſentiments of America.

C. S.

APPEN-

A P P E N D I X.

T H E two following Letters were first published in England in the Morning Post.

TO THE AUTHORS OF

THE REPUBLICAN.

GENTLEMEN,

M. DUCHASTELET has mentioned to me the intention of some persons to commence a Work under the title of *The Republican.*

As I am a Citizen of a country which knows no other Majesty than that of the People—no other Government than that of the Reprefentative body—no other Sovereignty than that of the Laws, and which is attached to *France* both by Alliance and by Gratitude, I voluntarily offer you my fervices in fupport of principles - as honourable to a nation as they are adapted to promote the happinefs of mankind. I offer them to you with the more zeal, as I know the moral, literary, and political character of thofe who are engaged in the undertaking, and find myfelf honoured in their good opinion.

But I muft at the fame time obferve, that from my ignorance of the French language, my works muft neceffarily undergo a tranflation; they can of courfe be but of little

utility,

utility, and my offering muft confift more
of wifhes than fervices—I muft add, that I am
obliged to pafs a part of this fummer in England and Ireland.

. As the Public has done me the unmerited
favour of recognizing me under the appellation of " Common Senfe," which is my ufual
fignature, I fhall continue it in this publication to avoid miftakes, and to prevent my being
fuppofed the author of works not my own. As
to my Political Principles, I fhall endeavour, in
this letter, to trace their general features in
fuch a manner, as that they cannot be mif-
underftood.

It is defireable in moft inftances to avoid
that, which may give even the leaft fufpicion
with refpect to the part meant to be adopted,
and particularly on the prefent occafion, where
　　　　　　　　　　　　　　　　　　a perfect

a perfect clearnefs of expreffion is neceffary to the avoidance of any poffible mifinterpretation. I am happy, therefore, to find, that the work in queftion is entitled " *The Republican.*" This word expreffes perfectly the idea which we ought to have of Government in general— *Res Publica*—the public affairs of a Nation.

F As to the word *Monarchy*, though the addrefs and intrigue of Courts have rendered it familiar, it does not contain the lefs of reproach or of infult to a nation. The word, in its immediate and original fenfe, fignifies *the abfolute Power of a fingle Individual*, who may prove a fool, an hypocrite, or a tyrant. The appellation admits of no other interpretation than that which is here given. *France* is therefore not a *Monarchy*, it is infulted when called by that name. The fervile fpirit which characterifes this fpecies of Government

vernment is banifhed from FRANCE, and this
country, like AMERICA, can now afford
to Monarchy no more than a glance of dif-
dain.

OF the errors which monarchic ignorance
or knavery has fpread through the world;
the one, which bears the marks of the moft
dexterous invention, is the opinion that the
fyftem of *Republicanifm* is only adapted to a
fmall country, and that a *Monarchy* is fuited,
on the contrary, to thofe of greater extent.
Such is the language of Courts; and fuch the
fentiments which they have caufed to be a-
dopted in monarchic countries; but the opinion is contrary at the fame time to principle
and to experience.

THE GOVERNMENT, to be of real ufe,
fhould poffefs a complete knowledge of all
the

the parties—all the circumſtances, and all
the intereſts of a nation. The monarchic
ſyſtem, in conſequence, inſtead of being
ſuited to a country of great extent, would
be more admiſſible in a ſmall territory,
where an individual may be ſuppoſed to
know the affairs and the intereſts of the
whole. But when it is attempted to extend
this individual knowledge to the affairs of a
great country, the capacity of knowing
bears no longer any proportion to the extent or multiplicity of the objects which
ought to be known, and the Government
inevitably falls from ignorance into tyranny.
For the proof of this poſition we need only
look to SPAIN, RUSSIA, GERMANY, TUR-
KEY, and the whole of the Eaſtern Conti-
nent—Countries for the deliverance of which
I offer my moſt ſincere wiſhes.

ON

On the contrary, the true *Republican* fyftem, by Election and Reprefentation, offers the only means which are known, and in my opinion the only means which are poffible of proportioning the wifdom and the information of a Government to the extent of a country.

The fyftem of *Reprefentation* is the ftrongeft and moft powerful center that can be devifed for a nation. Its attraction acts fo powerfully, that men give it their approbation even without reafoning on the caufe; and FRANCE, however diftant its feveral parts, finds itfelf at this moment *an Whole* in its *central* Reprefentation. The citizen is affured that his rights are protected, and the foldier feels that he is no longer the Slave of a Defpot, but that he is become one of the Nation, and interefted of courfe in its defence.

THE

THE States at prefent ftyled *Republican*, as HOLLAND, GENOA, VENICE, BERNE, '&c. are not only unworthy of 'the name, but are actually in oppofition to every Principle of a *Republican* Government, and the countries fubmitted to their power are, truly fpeaking, fubjected to an *Ariftocratic* Slavery!

IT is, perhaps, impoffible in the firft fteps which are made in a Revolution, to avoid all kind of error, in principle or in practice, or in fome inftances to prevent the combination of both. Before the fenfe of a nation is fufficiently enlightened, and before men have entered into the habits of a free communication with each other of their natural thoughts, a certain referve—a timid prudence feizes on the human mind, and prevents it from attaining its level, with that vigour and promptitude which belongs

to

to *Right*.—An example of this influence dif-
covers itfelf in the commencement of the
prefent Revolution:- but happily this difco-
very has been made before the Conftitution
was completed, and in time to provide a
remedy.

THE *Hereditary Succeffion* can never exift
as a matter of *right*; it is a *nullity*—a *nothing*. To admit the idea is to regard men
as a fpecies of property belonging to fome
individuals, either born or to be born! It is
to confider our defcendents, and all pofterity
as mere animals without a Right or a Will!
It is, in fine, the moft bafe and humiliating
idea that ever degraded the human fpecies,
and which, for the honour of Humanity,
fhould be deftroyed for ever.

THE idea of hereditary fucceffion is fo
contrary to the Rights of Man, that if we

F   were

were ourfelves to be recalled to exiftence, inftead of being replaced by our pofterity, we fhould not have the right of depriving ourfelves beforehand of thofe *Rights* which would then properly belong to us.   On what ground, then, or by what authority, do we dare to deprive of their rights thofe children who will foon; be men? Why are we not ftruck with the injuftice which we perpetrate on our defcendents, by endeavouring to tranfmit them as a vile herd, to mafters whofe vices are all that can be forefeen.

WHENEVER the *French* Conftitution fhall be rendered conformable to its *Declaration* of *Rights*, we fhall then be enabled to give to FRANCE, and with juftice, the appellation of a *civic Empire*; for its government will be the empire of Laws founded on the great republican principles of *Elective Reprefenta-*
tion,

tion, and the *Rights of Man* —But Monarchy and Hereditary Succeſſion are incompatible with the *baſis* of its conſtitution.

I hope that I have at preſent ſufficiently proved to you that I am a good Republican; and I have ſuch a confidence in the truth of theſe principles, that I doubt not they will ſoon be as univerſal in *France* as in *America*. The pride of human nature will aſſiſt their evidence, will contribute to their eſtabliſhment, and Men will be aſhamed of Monarchy.

I am, with reſpect

Gentlemen,

Your friend,

THOMAS PAINE.

LET-

LETTER

TO THE

ABBE SYEYES.

Paris, 8th July, 1791.

SIR,

"AT the moment of my departure for England, I read, in the *Moniteur* of Tuefday laft, your letter, in which you give the challenge, on the fubject of Government, and offer to defend what is called the *Monarchical opinion* againft the Republican fyftem.

" I ACCEPT of your challenge with pleafure; and I place fuch a confidence in the fuprioeirty of the Republican fyftem over that nullity of fyftem, called *Monarchy*, that I engage not to exceed the extent of
fifty

fifty pages, and to leave you the liberty of taking as much latitude as you may think proper.

" THE refpect which I bear your mora and literary reputation, will be your fecurity for my candour in the courfe of this difcuf fion; but, notwithftanding that I fhall trea the fubject ferioufly and fincerely, let m premife, that I confider myfelf at liberty to ridicule as they deferve, Monarchical abfur dities, whenfoever the occafion fhall prefen itfelf.

" BY Republicanifm, I do not under ftand what the name fignifies in Holland and in fome parts of Italy. I under ftand fimply a government by reprefentatio —a government founded upon the principle of the Declaration of Rights; principle

t

o'which feveral parts of the French Conftitution arife in contradiction. The Decla-
ations of the Rights of France and America
re but one and the fame thing in principles,
nd almoft in expreffions; and this is the
Republicanifm which I undertake to defend
gainft what is called *Monarchy* and *Ariſto-*
racy.

I SEE with pleafure, that in refpect to one
oint, we are already agreed; and *that*
s the extreme danger of a Civil Liſt of thirty
millions. I can difcover no reafon why one
f the parts of the government fhould be
upported with fo extravagant a profufion,
vhilft the other fcarcely receives what is fuf-
icient for its common wants.

" THIS dangerous and diſhonourable dif-
roportion, at once fupplies the one with
                                    the

the means of corrupting, and throws th
other into the predicament of being cor
rupted. In America there is but little dif
ference, with regard to this point, betwee
the legiflative and the executive part of ou
government; but the firft is much bette
attended to than it is in France.*

" In whatfoever manner, Sir, I may trea
the fubject of which you have propofed th
inveftigation, I hope that you will not doub
my entertaining for you the higheft efteen
I muft alfo add, that I am not the perfon:
enemy of Kings. Quite the contrary. N
man more heartily wifhes than myfelf to fe
them all in the happy and honourable ftat
of private individuals; but, I am the avow

* A Deputy to the Congrefs receives about a guinea and
half daily; and provifions are cheaper in America than
France.

ed, open, and intrepid enemy of what is called Monarchy; and I am ſuch by princi-ples which nothing can either alter or cor-rupt—by my attachment to humanity; by the anxiety which I feel within myſelf for the dignity and the honour of the human race; by the difguſt which I experience, when I obſerved men directed by children, and governed by brutes; by the horror which all the evils that Monarchy has ſpread over the earth excite within my breaſt; and by thoſe ſentiments which make me ſhudder at the calamities, the exactions, the wars, and the maſſacres with which Monarchy has cruſhed mankind: in ſhort, it is againſt all the Hell of Monarchy that I have declared war.

(Signed)   THOMAS PAINE."

THE END.

www.ingramcontent.com/pod-product-compliance
Lightning Source LLC
Chambersburg PA
CBHW021547270326
41930CB00008B/1398